The Phoenix

New & Selected Poems 2007 - 2013

I0148435

The Phoenix

New & Selected Poems 2007 - 2013

Judith Skillman

Dream Horse Press
Aptos, California

Dream Horse Press
Post Office Box 2080, Aptos, California 95001-2080

The Phoenix: New & Selected poems 2007 - 2013
Copyright © 2014 Judith Skillman
All rights reserved

No part of this book may be reprinted without the express written permission of the publisher. For permissions, contact Dream Horse Press, Post Office Box 2080, Aptos, California, 95001-2080. editor@dreamhorsepress.com

Printed in the United States of America
Published in 2014 by Dream Horse Press

ISBN 978-1-935716-32-7

Cover artwork:

Aloft
by Steven DeLuz,

stevendaluz.com

for my mother, Dr. Bernice Bloom Kastner

Contents

Tribal Moon Cycle

New Poems

"...and then at last there is the heart
where the dried bird itself
built a nest."

Lennart Sjögren, "The Bird"

from Coppelia, Certain Digressions

Dolls

Once they are horizontal
their eyes close—black lashes
fringing blue glass. If I were a mother
I'd want one of them
to sleep in a pile of leaves,
with a scarf around its neck.
If I had one it would never cry,
but lie empty as a cradle
while I pushed a metal swing.

I'm old and set in my ways
but if I had been in on the making
I would have taken the apple
and carved a mouth,
just by laying a knife into the light.

I'd have found the nose like a flat.
Letting myself in with the key
that becomes a shoe
I would never wake one up
and never be woken, but keep track
of how much younger I grew
just by pressing my cheeks
against fine-grained porcelain.

I'd have taken one to bed with me,
kept it warm in the hollow of my back
until its face crinkled
from the heat, its complexion melted.
I'd never lean over it

on the street, saying words that bloom
nerveless as grass, never tell it
what it already knows in its open arms
and absent heart to be true.

Coppelia

I.

Another autumn, days
and nights finally equal. She watches
the sun shrink to a sliver,
sees the first leaves swirl down
on their own.
Yesterday her arms seemed alive,
today she's nothing more
than a doll fixed on mechanical chores.

Was a single dawn worth waking to?
To come downstairs and set a pot
of water boiling. Was the egg
meant to harden in its shell,
leaving the yolk soft and yellow?

She had no mother to sing
like a lark, only a father building
his marionettes by legions in the basement.
When she sees through
her enamel eyes
is it true she can remember
Swanhilda, the woman her lover

left her for? Or can it be
she's proud to have them
strung together,
wooden in one another's arms.

II.

The man who made her wonders
which came first, his longing
to invest himself in a stick
woman, or his interest

in mechanical butterflies
that would fly around the room
like Samuel Hawthorne's,
each one more perfect than the last.

He wanders the streets,
watching grasshoppers leap
and fall back to asphalt.

III.

This is the doll, forever wooden,
brought by the air
to industry. Her arms
dangle from swept-back shoulders.

This doll is more complicated,
invested with shadow—
the gold's of an autumn
enriched with sorrow.

She stands on a balcony,
watches the drama
of a human woman
loved by a man.

The dowry she offers—
sanctuary of a lap
never molded by the head
of a child. Her arms trouble me

because no matter what I say
they refuse to draw in,
to round, to play a little ruse
called *ballet.*

Bruxism

If I am a happy animal who has landed
in a pile of leaves, it must be autumn.

It was my overly polite neighbor,
the night nurse, who stumbled and fell on ice.

It must be winter. Surfaces disappear
beneath drifts children marked as angels.

In crystals whole worlds shine.
Persistent illness is a natural occurrence.

This jaw's wired for some other Pollyanna.
I will not allow her angry forgiveness.

My mother was just grating carrots,

spicing her dishes with *asafetida* to hear the sizzle

of onions and veal. The same wind
holes up in a garret for an artist or a gourmet.

Whoever is lucky and lives in Paris
can look down on Hoffman's corner window.

If things are bad now they will get worse,
Hoffman said of an invalid's life.

His afternoon light, like coffee grounds,
lies stacked against buildings in this city old as taste.

Madame de D.

1.
Madame, the problem is restlessness.
My dowry's too low, yours is too high.
We will never marry the right man.
You're just seven, I'm forty-seven.
You carry the gene on the outside,
I have it here, under my skirt,
in my heart and a corkscrew of hair
escaped from the garish scarf.
We walk on opposite sides of the path
with Father between us, checking
to be certain it's you who flails
your arms. Show no fear, Madame.
At the base of this hill
water from the Straits of Juan de Fuca

licks cliffs as white as Dover.

2.

Madame de D., lay aside your fat yellow violin
on the bed, silly girl, who thinks
practice makes perfect. Scales and etudes,
arpeggio's and broken thirds,
for us the question's not one of repetition.
In every situation Father looms, like
the good doctor. An insidious business,
this laying the groundwork for secrets,
these words the springing to life from nowhere.
Women he has been with—
what do we care about the waitress from Toronto
he wishes he'd laid?
He and Doctor George Gilles de Tourette,
like you and I, Madame, owe our lives
to nothing more than a vanished order.
A series of dark notes, like wet leaves
climbing an ebony trellis.

3.

I'll punish you as I punished her, Madame de D.,
leaving the compass rose on her cheek,
denying and resisting,
finally sanctioning
the wreaths of high-pitched cries
by giving her something to cry about.
Your ringlets spiral like smoke rings
into the high-ceilinged cottage.
Good acoustics and bad genes,
the life of a solitary makes its demands,
Madame de D. Our disorders

have grown irresistible. Bad sleep,
like bad thoughts, can be stopped
by a switch. *Tsk tsk.*
Stop this mischief, picking flowers
for granny. Come on the count of three,
come to the yellow chair
and be still.
I know Madame can swallow her pills.
In your ironed hair
and starched white collar
you remind me of an expensive doll.

4.

A stubborn girl, I held you by one arm
and you screamed *no*, twisted
away from me, *pop.*
In the closet newborn chicks
murmured, balls of fluff.
Nursemaid's elbow, the good doctor said,
and put you back together. A joint
is like a lipstick. Tell me, Dr. Tourette,
can you make her stop these silly tricks?
Is she a piece of fancy or true imagination?
If fancy, why does she look at me
with glass-blue eyes?

5.

I love you, Madame, precisely
because you don't exist.
An unconditional love, like that of a mother
for her child. A century
has passed since you disgraced your family
by making those faces.

You who were never allowed to show fear
or think of white bears,
come here and sit with the grown ups.

6.

At the border of dream's a seam, Madame.
Mine it for all its worth.
Mother sits stitching in her chair.
Father turns circles clockwise,
counter-clockwise, checks doors
and windows. When the sounds begin—
obscene hissing, low notes
from the throats of animals—
exploit them, Madame,
as if they were your own.

The Sunflower

Stands taller than a man,
close to the roof of a house
that might have been Lotte's—
a houseful of children
with no mother.
Its leaves open to carry
whatever is left
in this bone-dry season
of clouded visions.
I suspect fatigue
lies at the bottom
of the well.
This flower: less than an aristocrat,
more than a serf.

Barely bourgeois,
like Goethe's *Werther*
when he went to take a court position.
Its single eye opens like the sun,
a Cyclops of tufted seeds the harvest
will never see.
Nothing comes to the one
who gazes up at a single flower
and wishes for treasure.
Jack climbed the beanstalk
and fell back to earth.
The sunflower—tower,
air castle, middle-aged star.

Reprisal

When I looked up
the titmouse had pecked its way
around a knothole
in the old oak.

I saw a telltale streak of gray
on its head, heard the syllable
it pronounced over and over,
a muted ululation.

There was delight in winter,
when seeds were scattered
by a loving hand in snow
to leave only a scar,

which the titmouse knew
how to interpret.

Why should I feel reproach each spring?
I thought of my father.

The moment of his death
happened over and over,
as if it were the only thing
that occurred in my lifetime,

like the Borges' character,
Emma Zunz. She had her methods
for revenge, but I had none,
unless to face

the house cat's blissful grin
when it left feathers on a door mat.
I knew in summer I'd find
wrens close at hand,

fallen from nests built
in forsythia and rhododendron
that grew like trees
in the unkempt yard.

Beatrice

If she blazes beside me,
I might turn to see
a face gone blue with light
from the moon.

If she honors the dead
I may wish for their return,
to finish a conversation,
if only with a ghost.

She sticks to me
like unfinished business,
her cloying presence
that of a celestial nun satisfied

with her lost station.
Under the wimple, in age
and desolation, I see her
more clearly, an apparition

shadowing my left shoulder.
If she wants to carry me
as she would a man,
still I am a woman.

And though the seas
of earth and moon
are lifeless, filled with young men
who died in their prime,

she continues forever
her botched attempts to mother.
Beatrice, like Mary,
a mother figure steeped in platitudes.

A Pollyanna full of proverbs.
A dominatrix, this woman—
so full of sensuality
it was easy to outshine

visions of Paradise,
those poor souls
forever cloistered outside
the white-petaled rose of the godhead.

But Beatrice lied.
When she turned her face
she blinded Virgil.
Where can she stand to live,

this whorish heroine
who stacked apartments
until they became tenements
ripe with the scent

of concupiscence drying,
habitats full of young love,
garbage, white noise,
and cigarettes.

Procustes' Bed

His merciless hospitality
has served her well.
She approaches the inn,
sees a light shining like a city star,
goes inside.

There are two beds.
She no longer knows
whether to lie on the larger one
and be stretched,
or take the smaller
and have her feet lopped off
at the ankles.

Short of that,
there are only questions.
Why the rigidity of Spring,
birds fastened to trees,
the almond still insisting
it's a rose? She'd prefer
to be at table with him,
in conversation.

Red or white, she'd raise
her glass to his
and hear the crystal clink.
Does the shy Narcissus
infect a room with scent
before it nods and falls?

She knows at least
here she'll be taken care of,
the past with its inimitable
posture of deceit
allowed a memory.

She removes her hat and scarf.
Sometimes there's only one bed.
Then it is a better myth,
one left up to him.

The first delicate shoots
redden and shy away
from trees outside a window
paled by dawn or dusk,
and no one near
to see him carry her
across the threshold, like a bride.

from Anne-Marie Derèse & The Green Parrot

Green Parrot

I saw a parrot in the ficus.
Heard it talking in sentences.
I have grown bizarre in this boa.
Crackers for a time of war.
Policemen guarded the hotel.
The parrot was immaculate
on foreign soil,
and if the eye saw us looking,
it did not tell. There was no inquisition,
no history to be rewritten.
Only the depths of a water
at times taupe, black, or turquoise.
The yachts departed lazily
with their rummies,
and we stayed behind,
holding inadmissible evidence
that someone's pet
had been abandoned to language
in the vagaries
of a Mexican afternoon.

Near the John Huston Restaurant

The beach is replaced by dump trucks
filled with sand, their loads deposited
in a noisy secrecy like women rejoicing
over the end of a war.
Men occupy their nights
with shots of the best tequila

from bottles with worms at the bottom.
A waiter named *Ramone* feeds
a grackle. He clucks and the bird
with the yellow eye comes to him in the café.
Ramone donates leavings from a plate,
he points proudly
at his pet grackle's blue-black plumage,
its feathers like Elizabeth Taylor's hair.
Someday, he says, his silver teeth flashing,
I eat this bird. The hotel doesn't feed
anyone or anything. It takes from
the monied hand, it shines
a ribbon of kitsch—trumpets and lights.
Beneath white-washed arches a stage appears
in pinks and purples to frame dancers
on Tuesday nights, those who entertain
the rich old ones with spotted faces.
If the day has gone to a new home
across the Pacific, passing its fine lineage
to an infinity of islands,
still the night stays on—an iguana
from a movie whose figurehead has vanished.

A Palm Tree

The shroud of Turin peels away
Beneath green globes
That hold all the milk
Left on earth.
This is the shell a man will crack
Against a rock.

Rain-white sky pours into sand
Effects the sea made
When it climbed by centimeters
Higher on the beach
To expose roots.
Palms sway
Beneath a palapa
Made from a palimpsest
Of leaves.
Earth stiffens
As if ready to fall
Into hot coals,
Where already the fish head
Grins on its skewer.

Bougainvillea

Bright as women who wash by hand.
These blossoms lay claim
To a specific act—flowering—
Though they are only leaves.
Then, one per hour,
They fall to lie like white moths
Or crimson umbrellas a waiter places
In tropical drinks.
Unable to move or breathe,
Kerchiefs not yet defiled
By the gracelessness
Of humanity.

Pigeons

When they croon on banisters
outside her room, it reminds her
of the infants, crying, forever
half asleep and half awake.

The infants were always there
for her, needing what she could give—
her breast, voice, and scent.
In this, her second life, a switch

has flipped. The city lies
within reach. It holds nothing
she wants except the iridescent green
bibs on the pigeons, their incessant

preening, their desire for crumbs.
In this, the other story, she never married,
never carried or cared for anyone.
Terra cotta pots and red shingled roofs—

the shadows sharpened
near dusk along the wharf.
Far away they could see Alcatraz.
For accompaniment, the small heads

and plump bodies followed along,
as if obedience were easy.
The pigeons rested on cement to dupe her,
to deliver the cooing that would lull her

to sleep. She dreamt she was a girl.
Seconds later, an old woman.
No matter. She still has books,
pens, pills, a carton of milk, and sugar.

It's not so bad to shelve the past.
It's not her fault, to have been born
of stock too meek,
too gentle for this world.

Pie Bird

Mother summoned flour into a ball,
rolled her anger out on a board,
sprinkled it with water,
and pleated pastry with her thumbs.

A pie bird entered the oven—
its belly hollow to allow steam to escape.
Blackbird with a yellow beak,
a bit of crust stuck fast.

All night the child dreamt
of watery horses. Horses gaunt
and useless, worse than paper cut-outs.
Ponies she couldn't mount or ride,

bridles of criss-crossed leather straps.
Metal bits fitted to the swollen folds
of their mouths. The pink tongues
always working up foam,

as if to queer the bit
that would have to be endured
like the future, a blank space,
a plain stretched taut as hunger.

Berries whisked with sugar,
sweetness followed by a sick feeling
in the gut. Spoon that swatted flies,
burst bubbles, and held onerous stains.

While Mother worked
the counter, the child sweated.
Drops on her forehead
rolled down the book

she pretended to know how to read.
Who knows the prayers
of a girl caught for years
in a summer kitchen.

Quizno

If you want to know more
About the lizard Mexicans call *quizno*
Pick it up, watch it dart back
Along white stucco
While you hold the tail
Still writhing in your hand.

from Prisoner of the Swifts

Newborns

They prickle my dreams
this life come from and forthcoming

always making remaking itself
out of the stubborn itch of an insect.

They make a breach in the disease of death
when they come out on the gurney

after fermenting in bed in a great wealth of pain.
They expose the milk for what it is

and the breast for its function.
How well intercept waking and falling asleep

masquerading as unity, divinity
in their bare outfits as if the Buddha himself

where born again and had forgotten how to behave.
The stork's been busy with his beak

I ask the policeman and how? Very well
he replies and when they come

I dream badly of them as if they were two cockroaches
we ordered from torn menus

in the age we were given and at the appointed time.
They emerge covered in sacs of cheese cloth

torn from their mother too early
like shards of glass or beaks twittering

under the skin and inside the ear it happens
like the early hours always too small.

If they are sisters they clatter
if brothers their grim dignity unbearable

if figments of a repetitive nightmare
that part finishes where the highway ends underwater.

We put them into tubs,
launching their restless energy.

Reeds hide us from those
who would take the newborns away from us

but it's we they've put into the boats.
The sky is dawning faintly

as we say good bye to the territories
and our bathtub bobs out on the river.

We hear their ululations from the bank—
shush...

Not the Quantity But the Quality

In the afternoon our passion
is like cinnabar. More color
than taste. At night passion
· is like chalk, less than we wanted
but enough to show through
faintly, like the outline

of your jaw now you've shaved
your beard. In the morning
you are gone again, a man
I've lived with thirty years
and seven, off and on living
as if we were married
with and without the passion,
bound to earth by law
and to one another
by the knowledge that death,
like passion, comes first to one
and then to the other.

Another Winter

after Jehuda Amichai

The pain-people have returned
from their countryside—
fog, gray, and cold.
They finger bare branches
and turn up in waking dreams.

The pain-people have come back
with words in their mouths
to ask me to join them.
A few months is not so bad,
they say, *come home.*

But the countryside—
how am I to survive
even a few months
within these barren grounds.
The weather is prison enough—

gun-metal sky, off-gray place
not worth looking around in
for what's gone cold and hard
as a dead star. Off-color jokes
and gossip like slander.

The pain-people run raw fingers
across barren trees—Big-Leaf Maple,
Cherry the crows picked clean,
Dogwood with blood-red branches.
The say words that sound like *vote*.

Of all my waking dreams
this is the worst. I pace, holding
what I can of pleasure to my chest—
baby bucking in the throes of colic,
memory of the sun up high.

A Late Elegy

Almost December. A shock of blue
shoots from the hydrangea I planted
in memory of my father the astronomer—
his ashes, his stars.

Only one bloom this year.
Still it rises above black leaves
fallen from the apple tree,
whose naked limbs nod in assent.

The colorless branches trouble me.
I dream unripe dreams.
A stiff wind returns to the cul-de-sac
bringing its news—wax logs, sirens,

and cigarette smoke. I hear the whippoorwill
that should have left in autumn
but stayed on instead to winter in the yard.
I recognize this nocturnal, insect-eating nightjar.

I can't say which coast I'm on,
east or west, only that the water
has made inroads. Whippoorwill—its name echoes
its cry. The Jew who chose to be cremated

instead of buried, the man who could never
forgive himself despite all he overcame.
Poverty, stigma, the present of a broken pen
to his best friend when he was just a boy.

I fasten pearls around my neck,
my diamonds sparkle like his stars.
It's not so bad to be haunted by a nightjar
stuck to an apple tree. To be singular, or rich.

I watch the planets rise—Jupiter
with feathered bars, Saturn's mechanical rings.
The red shoulder and blue heel
of Orion tell me it is winter,

soon enough the doves will be driven,
like little sisters, from the sky above the gingko.
So what if my past
is prehistoric, if it nods and poses

above leaves cut in patterns,
yellow swans stuck to the earth.
What's left of my father—a hydrangea bloom
refusing to brown nose the cold.

Prisoner of the Swifts

As out of a fever dream
        they dart,

                pleat,

                        tuck,

hem me in—

                swifts

        hurling

                like shrapnel fragments

                        from nests

        spun of their own sputum.

                All day

spent in my own company,

                        that invalid

companion who no more wants

                                to be

released

from her cell

                than a nun

cloistered,

        fed bread and water

                through a rust-latched door.

        All day

                sequestered

by their aeronautics,

                the *apous*—

depicted by medievalists

              as without feet,

     short-legged,

         never settling.

     Soundlessness

made visible by speed,

         a flicker

the eye sees

     through floaters,

       myopia,

         the swayback

ground

       of progressive lenses.

To mate on the wing,

         to be airborne

   in cartwheel,

        round-off,

back handspring—

      once

   I could do these things.

   All day

gnawed from the inside out

   as my quick-witted

wardens

       circle the house

        with whispers.

They make of clear air a facsimile—

         thin-veined,

    opaque

   and impassable as brocade.

The Body Especial

I said I had almost forgotten about the sick.
Their glazed eyes, their little fevers are spawning
the same conclusions. We go in, and the day
yawns open, white pieces of sky pinned back.

A room. It always begins in a space
with a narrow table. Here are the eminent
details—the useless magazines,
acres of acoustic ceiling, and squares
of gauze that wait for tongs and silence.

But it wasn't there, exactly. Although
it began there, and took on the heartbeat
of arrhythmia, due, we speculated,
to a gratuitous electric shock.
I remember leaping backwards.
Epiphany took me by the shoulders,
no less.

I say it began there. And changed, overnight
to black pockets of fluid, caught up, dire,
needy—those places in the second body
I carried.

*

El Nino comes again with its red spot, a bruise,
a septicemia clinging to the coast,
bringing this rabid girl with it. Her hair
is tangled, so I lean in close, thinking
I'll study the overlapping strands, and finally
decipher the rat's nests.

The child throws pills at me and wanders off
into a dream. A version of herself,
ripe with cysts and strong urine.
Samples leak from odd containers

until she spawns a sister
who grows an anomaly when her ovaries
kick in—*size of a mandarin orange,*
we were lucky—these words
spoken underwater, by a surgeon
in green.

Morning Glory

Because it entwines other plants,
because it was brought here from another coast,
like jimson and scotch broom,
it should be pulled.

Small wild things surrender
to its tendrils.
It chokes whatever it engages.
I dreamt of entanglement—

white flowers opening at dawn
and closing at dusk.
The silent treatment is peculiar
when it occurs near water.

My husband pounds an espalier
against the house. A single Gravenstein,
blotched black, floats in the bowl
with store-bought fruit.

Spasmodic Torticollis

It sounded
like an Italian dish,
something with artichokes,
fresh bell peppers,
curvy pasta and asparagus,
not a malady. The doctor said,
It happened while you slept
face down on one side
for too long...
I felt like a horse
in blinders—unable to turn
toward the pain
of an excruciating
street scene.
When I tried to glance
over my shoulder
at the younger self
who watched
me from shadow,
I held the rigid posture
of a schoolmarm
who would not listen
to a tattletale, no matter
what the story.
It was as if a stiff,
uncompromising widow
had replaced me.
Where was the hapless,
disorderly sleep
of that younger woman
who had, with her easy manners

and the breath of her sexiness,
for too many years
eluded me.

Early August

The stars have given all they can
and now leaves take over the sky.
The big leaf maple, its tyranny
of years and useless harvests.

The doubled trunk, flexible
as rubber in a storm, quieted
by breezes, as peanuts scattered
for the squirrel are eaten by the raccoon.

It was summer in our bones
and the sky continued to wax and wane
like the moon—a crescent, where before
a pocked face shone with reflected light.

The sound of shells broken and flung,
the husk that holds a soul—whatever
angel-daemon comes and goes is gone.
The stars have cooled and taken on

their proper colors—blue for Rigel,
red for Betelgeuse. Aldeberan,
the eye of the bull, redder still.
Sirius, the dog star, a rumor

that warmed the earth in summer
for the ancients, recedes behind a Cherry
picked clean by crows. Early
and earlier it comes back to us, our denial,

our shock at the stories we hear,
the truth grown up like the relative
we knew as a child—the one who watched
over us, molested us, and let us go.

Daphne

Could be the name of a girl,
or a mythic goddess
who carries her immortality
like loneliness.

Her green legs,
her fluted lips, and that scent—
too sweet for the unbeautiful
to believe in.

I imagine I caress a woman,
woman myself. Such delicate
parts, the labile self
opening as if to the male hummingbird

with its red iridescent ruff...
I imagine I am her lover,
Daphne, the one who,
lonely for another, can take on

anyone, adore anyone, make love
to either sex
as if the hermaphrodite
were the original Narcissus, who stood

outside the window
or hovered above the lake
watching wing beats accrue. For Daphne,
there is no present, past, or future.

When I come to her,
she wears the flimsiest of all my selves.
She places her green hand in mine.
I swallow her composure.

When we leave we take with us
the perfect measure of correctness,
full-grown now like the shadow
of thunderheads to the west.

Our Hero

His birth attended by oracles,
he ends up in a reed basket,
swaddled in the infant's jar-like body.
His mother launches him.

If the river's a ribbon he's found later,
his surrogate parents happier
than they were before.

If the sea is full of whitecaps, sirens,
milfoil, or chop, he drowns,
only to become a snake
in orange mud, a changeling.

He wanders into the hinterlands
against the wishes of his false parents
to seek out his father.

He'll lie, murder,
do whatever is necessary
to make a proper end of the story,
the one we carry deep in our bones.

It's a wonder we don't recognize
him before the amulet, badge, purple
heart has been nailed to his chest.

Christ, Mohammed, Moses—so many names
they make us dizzy. We dress, celebrate,
fête this makeshift god who thrives
on our need for a hero so good
he got to be bad.

Bending to Work in the Heat

                    Rows and columns,
the corn raising its silk tassels in august ceremony,
my mother tethered to her shovel,
breaking red Maryland clay
          into chunks.

Nothing single in that garden—
flies, and their cousins,
          the horseflies—
bees, and their sisters,
          the wasps.

The sun spawned
    a twin
   in milk-blue sky.
I remember what needed to be tended—
dirt, virgin zucchini and tomatoes.

       In pure solicitous warmth
the heat became our primer.
We absorbed its thirsts and irritations,
its longings. I stepped on a hornet.
My gloveless hands found worms
   halved by mother's shovel.

Maternal garden, garden
where Adam and Eve
   melted into one another,
their arms and legs entangled
like the morning glory.
Whatever the heat wanted it took.

The sun fell into the Potomac by degrees.
A moon rose, cold to the touch—
   pink quartz, exotic dessert.

We were tamped by father's anger,
quelled by punishments
like the earth in mother's garden.

Drip of a casement air conditioner
that whet more than cooled
the starts of smooth, white breasts
   hung on the bones of our chests.

Breath Hunger

As if she were at altitude,
the air thin and cold.
A dilution, a lack.
The same kind of dread
as a death rattle.
Mornings, when she ran uphill,
the trees were swollen
with oxygen. Branches reached
toward her, tentacles
like the octopus.
She was afraid of bright orange,
of what waited on the culvert
along the spit
in the drowning place.
There, below the water line,
etched on steel,
was the tell—
tidal highs and lows
driven by the full moon.
She picked tiny crabs
like berries from metal.
Held them at arm's length
and watched their legs beat,
miniature pincers
nipping at nothing.
Thought she would like
to hold the octopus
in her mind like a question.
There was nothing
but the bloating
of all that was not hers.
She envied those

who could breathe freely,
laugh, yawn, call the earth home.
Even the *chela*
had its grasp,
the claw its largesse.

More Tenderly

She thinks of bird song
not as insufferable,
but as the scraping shut
of a door.

Each drilled note
no more than an echo
of what was said
in the house of childhood.

If thirty years remain intact,
she's not less surprised
than when she returns to a duet
and finds, among the untouched

places in her mind,
clouds and ribbons
set far back in the sky.
The distance between then

and now a kind of pain
she forages through,
making sounds
that sound like moans

but aren't. She thinks
the proof of love is exhaustion.
That she's tired
but not tired enough.

Nature Morte

The orange sports
a bit of green-tinged cobalt
on its skin. A few bananas
malinger, spotted, oversweet
          in the oval bowl.

A crystal cup passed down
like the ages—some things
never go away.
Kiwis toy with *Delicious*
apples, their nets ripped open.
          In the background

a bottle bleeds its own shadow
to make room for the sensual.
And here—at precisely this juncture—
the light sits shining
its sign for number:
          titanium white.

One senses the horror
in the life of fruits. Seedless grapes
shaped like teeth, forgiven
their onerous temptation,
to which grandfather
          succumbs.

Does he hate the infant's cloying,
sticky fingers plastered
against his stolid jaw,
his planed face? For he
is not endeared
        to this painting.

Seam
                for Erika

Before the cutter
laid his fabric
out on long tables,
before his wife
chased the runner duck,
tall and sleek,
around its filthy pen
and slit its throat
to let the blood run clean,
before you or I came
to be fifty-four,
there were others
whose hands
held fronts to backs,
measured, chalked,
cut, and notched.
Those for whom
a yard of cloth
would become,
by dint of necessity,
only clothes. Your hands
on the feed dogs,

mine on the keyboard.
Let the sheep
be shorn, the ducks
be plucked, the sheers
be hung. We owe
our ancestors
these renderings
of a present
filled with the *joie de vivre*
they toiled to give us.
Your bright handiwork
and extravagant flowers
sewn into place,
their songs sung again
as whispers within
linen-colored walls.

Witch Hazel

Liquid amber.
The day, its pliant sun.
I remember inflammation,
the bruise-colored blood
of sunset.

Those days are gone.
A bit of rust
clings to the horse trailer.
I walk the same beat
from house to lake

and back again,
past the same chimes,
melodies wrung by wind
until they want
to resolve.

Do they haunt you,
her horses,
her dressage and eventing—
could you stand and watch her
take the three-foot jumps?

Left with impressions
the other life,
its fullness
and the carriage
of her children's heads—

left behind—an extract—
a woman becomes seasonless,
childless, emptied
even of evil, but for
bark, beads, and spikes.

November Moon, Past Full

Pours its dead, mimetic light
upon the lilac, that shrub still posing
like the manikin of foliage
as if it were summertime.
Moonlight on the witch hazel,

which was ugly before and then again,
just after flowering. It was summer
so soon and then it was over.
She wants to be taken in, to be as gullible
as before, but something has ebbed
in her. She feels no resistance to the past
and no anticipation for the future.
Knows the present long ago ceased
to exist—how plastic the words were,
how evanescent the vowels that taught
themselves to talk on her tongue.
If she worries too much, and her breath
grows shallow, the moon could fall to earth.
It would hurtle through the window
without warning,
just as every other ball
to left field came close to her mitt
and then fell back to earth, scents
of grass and leather caught in her hair.

from The Never

The Crinolines

In cages readied beside water,
in crab pots dropped from the rowboat
where an oar bleeds into an oarlock, from
land and water they come—
farthingale, petticoat, pannier.

If it is difficult to hold the umbrella steady
under rain that sheets,
think of the woman who enters the carriage
as if she were the first one
to wear the newfangled cloth of reform.

She stands, feet planted beneath
her shoulders as if she were ready
to take on the gods of satire
in a heady gust of wind.
The crinolines are burning, in lumber

piled beside a well-stocked
garage, in crinolettes and gadgetry
of the last century piled haphazardly
one on the other. In cotton
that smells of sweat and horses,

in nylon bearing the stain of blood.
The bride stands on her pedestal
wearing a bustle that has returned
for its chance to bear
the brunt of history.

Doppelganger

You there in the corner—
say a word or two.
Throw us something
to chew on, some grass
or a slender reed
we might blow on
until the tones rise
and enter our bones
like a Tibetan prayer bowl
rimmed by a bamboo stick.
Hey you two, members
of the clan of the unborn—
come here and answer
for what you've done.
What, mirror images?
One left-handed, one right?
One parochial, one secular?
It was the zygote split
you into clones. In June
the lilac rusts, blossom-heads
welded like Siamese twins.
June and the wild cherry
drops stems for lack of bees
to pollinate the sweets.
It's not enough
not to be annihilated
by a vision. Nor do we
wish to carry our bodies
forward against the blunt
weather told by a map

empty of all but symbols.
How could we envy what
we never had? Admit
that hunger will be your
demise. Grow infantile.
Slip from your mother
one at a time,
bound by a cord,
fed by the bloody
sun and moon
stuck in orbit
around one another.

A Foreign Beer Garden

Wherever there were poor,
there were pelicans.
Laundry strung on lines in the rain.
I remember the scoop and swallow,
the smile of a widow and her daughter
setting tables in an outdoor restaurant.
Later the chairs stood on their front legs in a warm rain,
the tablecloths were folded, their flowerings
bizarre as the hot pepper envelope
in which sheets of cheese melted.
I remembered being poor and hot,
hearing my Mother mention stone soup.
At night vivid imaginings.
Grasshoppers crossed my pillow, crickets sang
from embankments. Don't think the sea forgets

what it carries—a resemblance, a blank stare
and then, once more, the waiter with one eye
standing before our table, asking about drinks.

Serum Sickness

By the time she sits down
it is already late,
well into the syrup-colored skies
of another autumn.
The leaf of basil she picked
to scent olive oil
almost overpowers her.
Chrysanthemums, purchased
as an afterthought with a bag of groceries,
have spindled out of hand.
Low brow grapes wince
as they creep, still green,
along their trellis—
a length of chain link
behind the convenience store.
To be watered on a whim
is the same as
being watered too much.
To be ogled, handled, squeezed—
it all amounts to a case of nerves.
She dawdles on the porch,
watches for the squirrel,
that prankster
who became her master last summer.
By the time her body realizes it's been had—

too many antibodies in the blood—
it's too late to take back
grimaces, words, and arguments
enhanced by low-grade fever.
She eyes the polish on her nails—
Nantucket Pink this week,
toned down like the season.
Still wet, glistening
like a syringe
with the gleam of overkill.

Hot and Cold

Lucretius knew
the middle ground
was all a man could see.
The extremes would make
a person go mad—
hypothermia,
where the snow becomes
a soft bed of down,
has claimed the best climbers.
In the heat
of a closed-up place
an old woman dies
from the same dream
that made life exciting
when she was young.
We are caught
off balance,
trying to right ourselves

when it snows in April.
Summer lasts
past late-October,
the rose puts out one more
Lincoln bloom.
We don't think to question
the laziness in our heads,
floaters rising and falling
like dance gnats
in our retinas.
We know enough
not to ask
for more than this world,
its twinned blossoms
of flower and snow—
its feverish kisses,
powdered masks,
whirling dervishes
and incestuous whims.

The Sister

First-born in every version
of the story.
Even as a twin
she came first.
The hard pushes
were for her.
She grew faster,
ate more and better,

turned over first,
walked on quadriceps.
And yes, she was jealous.
Used her sibling as a crutch,
pushing the dark head down
to raise herself
a notch higher.
They played in the grass
until the grab and shove
turned the younger sister,
the one born
with its curse—
that once-mild child
chorused full-throated shrieks.
The cat ran,
the dog shied away
from Cain's pig-squeals
and fat, fur-laced fingers.
Cain grew weedy.
She hid in the laurel hedge.
Her sharp nails,
like morning glory
blooms, spiraling
chokeholds.
And those seeds—
hallucinogenic—
she shook six into her palm
before choosing her weapon.

Death of Pan

We were only playing in the pasture,
wearing a patchwork of sun and sky,
ragged with the coming autumn.
That is to say we didn't mean
to drown out the sound of his flute—
our piper, nor meddle with the conch shell
that caused our fathers to panic.

And his Arcadia—
how we adored her. We made wreaths
of wildflowers, twined tendrils of her hair
around our stubby hands as we brought
her one more gift: a leaf bloodied with color,
a spare sapling, an agate choked in quartz.

Until the river-god,
happy as ever to be plunged in cold,
took him from our arms and flung
his instrument against the rocky shore.
The syrinx shattered into seven reeds or nine,
and we, still infatuated with the echoes
our voices made in that valley, called out
to one another, not so much from loneliness
as the excitement of recitation.

Light breezes
dog us as we go forward in reconnaissance,
teaching one another how to suffer
being schooled by lechers. Our appetite
for the one called *Pitys*—another nymph
loved by him, who turned into a pine tree
to escape his overtures,
runs nil to none.

Dodo Bird

with lines from Hölderlin

I found it land-bound, small wings tucked
against its sides. The head naked,
almost human in its appraisal.
I remember hearing about you, I said
and it replied *For the gods grow indignant...*

It was not repulsive, rather oily, a few black strands
like leftover feathers sprouting from its head.
I thought you were a figment I said,
and it replied *if a man not gather himself to save His soul...*

I said I was a woman, that I would have preferred
to lose the ostrich, but would not starve my children.
If there had been a famine and the opportunity arose
I also would have beaten the Dodo to death
with whatever was at hand—
club, baseball bat, plank of wood,
but I wouldn't have laughed.

Women are tame.
We don't kill unless threatened.
Did you not perceive the Dutchmen as a threat?
Yet he has no choice...
the bird replied, foraging, head down,
diamond eyes shrunken to slits
as it pried grubs from mud.

Why have you grown so large—
three feet tall, walking about
as if you owned the ground
between clouds of idealism and germs of reality.
You had your heyday.

We have your beak in the British Museum
for proof: DNA, some writings and renderings.

It went about the business of the omnivorous—
scavenging, turning its *arse* this way and that,
always the silly walk of it
and the precious non-birdness of its serious demeanor,
unshaken by extinction: *like-*
wise; mourning is in error...

From the Grasslands

We came to an ocean paved with clouds.

Entered the remains of a forest.

Found strands of green coiled around rock.

The serpent lived here just as in the past.

We walked lightly, our shoes stained with meadows.

The quarter moon hung in daylight.

Iodine on a wound.

The sea boiled carbon dioxide stew.

Both manta ray and angel fish were gone.

An oasis changed from blue to a shade we did not know.

We stopped trying to drink bits of rainwater we'd collected on our tin roofs.

Ducts swollen shut from disuse.

The myths died and settled at our feet like elephant seals.

Our clothes wore more deeply than our dreams.

The sun came out of hiding to redden our skin.

It was then that the world caught fire.

Those Bleeding Hearts

Well, naturally
they would have to go before the others.
Not after the lion, chimpanzee, zebra, or giraffe.
Certainly not post-monkey
and dog gangs roaming the streets
of an exiled city.

You could go so far as to say
endangerment would be endemic
to a species whose heart was located
by a red mark suspiciously like blood,
or by the sort of folk
who are overly sympathetic to lost causes—
those island birds, liberals, and ground doves.

They would have to be killed off.
If not by the exact spot
at which to take aim with a shotgun,

then by their own inbred ability
to ooze sap, juice, and pink heart-shaped flowers.
Their pilfering predicated on a tendency
to fall victim to extortion.
To be trimmed, to run together, to seep through
the covers, as in, stain.

Even to feel grief, pain, or other
equally splashy stubs of emotion
that might be later expanded upon
follows too closely upon the heels
of another animal—sentimentality.

What about the vivid red color
splashed across white breasts?
This is no time to wax precious
about their alleged disappearance.
We have heard rumors of sightings.

These bits of gossip and bleeps
have not been recorded with any certainty.
Who would want to give away
the location of that which lies outside the margin,
in the peaceable kingdom beyond pastoral boundaries.

Extinction's Cousin

I came back for scraps—
      what else could I carry in my dislocated jaw?

With my tough, oily flesh,
      what chance would I have of finding relatives?

I came for a theory.

String theory, combustion theory.
A shred of evidence:

"So, in an unsettling Damien Hirst-like tableau, the bird was beak to beak
with its own face…"

I knew allusions would be required.

Illegible notes,
the certain rustling of papers
unearthed as the dead make peace with the living,

that I must wait a considerable length of time,

as after a bereavement.

It has been that long.
Here I stand before you wearing just plain skin.

What name will you give me,

the one without fur, scales, or feather?

What will you say to a second extinction?

I came to the island of trash, Mauritius, near Madagascar, where
there are certain butterflies and jewels left among corrugated roofs
and contraptions to siphon rainwater into buckets that reek with
odorous sulphurs.

I was looking for a fluke.

Perhaps the Dodo bird.

Give me something endemic to the landscape—

no palms, no sugarcane.

Allow me a shell, a bit of coral with some color left in
it,
mauves that exist only in the imagination.

Can we name those we never knew?

Of the fragmentary Oxford Dodo, shopworn
and foul-smelling,

only articles from *Nature*
and DNA survive.

Let's sift through the passenger pigeon's leavings,
its calling cards and mother-of-pearl wings.

Are these our relatives?

What do they say
when they gather together
for feasting?

What say when breaking a crust of rock to aid the
search
of a revered specialist, a man

who has traveled beyond tourism
and hard candy

to satisfy his eccentric needs for pelican tooth.

How will we deal with fossilized pollen?

How excavate shit, mine mud, dig out

        glacial till to find a bone.

I came back for this—
"a great fowle somewhat bigger than the largest Turky cock."

    I came to the circus to see
        one Dodo who had survived its water passage to

        the British Isles.

The absurdly large bill frightened me into silence.

Wheatlands

To travel is to dream of wheat,
passing over and under the drape
and pleat of hill and valley, darts taken in
when floodwaters passed over the earth.

To dream is to revel in scenery,
to be nourished by land—its crop tarnished
by harvest, like the stubble on a man's face
that makes the face handsome to a woman.

To sleep is to travel inside the germ
and the chaff. To wake is to breathe
a fine dust rising, bedeviled.

To dream is to become the whirling dervish
stuck inside the golden hen—
that one—who clucked at us
about hysteria until the day she died.

Our journey takes a year, a week, a day,
or an hour. Roads the color of wood smoke
cross fields. A water table lies thirty feet down,
under soil thicker than flourless cake.

In drought, dun-colored pyramids
grow from the mouths of machinery.
Sun beats down on the Palouse.

We come to savor this crop grown brighter
than noon, poorer than dusk.
A whole hell full of dollars gone blank as a page.

We comb the fields with our eyes,
picking out threads of silence,
choosing the nap and the grain.
Prefer gold, the land says, and we do.

The *Never*

They lie in separate rooms while the moon
spills its light across limbs of trees.
The fake owl poses in the yard next door—
those yellow eyes she saw and thought
it was a Great Horned Owl. The *never*
comes in spurts, like wings across the kitchen
skylight cutting her off from him
during the day. *Never* takes the form of sleep
at night. It's not that *never* belongs

to no one else. Practically anyone
could be happy under the sentence of moon
on gravel, moon on frost, moonlight
on fake owl perched in a willow.
Perhaps the moon is birch wood, she thinks,
and it was part of the *never* before this never.
Maybe the wings are obsidian and covered
the skylight when a piece of the Kuiper Belt
exploded above their house. Inside she feels
a bit like *never*. Likes the sound of mingling
with folks that might live there. Likes the fake owl,
who never asks *who*.

An Invitation

Come inside where it's warm
and I'll take off your past
like a jacket. Come sit by the fire
and feel for the last five-dollar bill
in your pocket. Watch it curl and burn,
lend a bit of turquoise to color
       the flame.

Come in from the woods,
from the paper mill, the sumptuous odor
of whatever it is you've been making
along with atrocity. You must know
I have been waiting for your arrival.
You must feel the stain of my hand
on your arm, see the bit of beard I've grown,
despite my being, or having been,
       a woman.

Come inside. There are potatoes
with poisonous eyes and apples gone soft
at the middle. I've seen what you do
with your life and I forgive you. I've met
the middleman and forgiven him. When
you and I go together to meet whomever
is waiting for us—can you hear
the saxophone wailing, the little train
            without a caboose...

When we find ourselves at the end
it will be in the rain or beside the sea.
When we're gone, the same dull rain
will fill an impartial sea. Only our feet
will be cold, the gray leather soles of us
like two stiffs out for a night on the town,
naked except for
            our blue toes.

Biopsy

Not so much
            the Lidocaine's
eager bee sting,

nor the narrow needle
            probing her left breast
to aspirate fluid
            from the carrot-shaped dark
found by ultrasound.

Not pain per se—
            rather what follows.

The barrel-shape vial
            and honey-thick fluid
marked with her name
            and date of birth.

No, not the stinging,
            nor the dull ache
that inhabits the hive
            of her breast
afterwards.

The problem lies
            in the vocabulary
of pathology.

Ducts trail
                        string-like
patterns on film,
                        worm
their way back
            to the inverted nipple
she found while standing nude
            before the same mirror
that gave her middle-age,
            grand-motherhood, and dread.

In situ, intra-ductal,
            ectasia, hyperplasia, carcinoma...

She couldn't feel
　　　more like a hostage
were she to don
　　　the bee's jacketed stripes,
the garb of the jail.

Feeder

How many secrets
were bequeathed to the earth
by its needle-beak—
that *poseur*, the hummingbird,
playing at a feeder
of sweetened water
a widow placed before her window
even after the wild currant
　　　had bloomed.

Epilogue

Rain all day off and on
and to be stuck in a cottage
by the sea, a path leading down
to the lighthouse, a path leading up
to the site of fortresses
graffiti'd now, roofs open to sky,
sheaves of goats beard
slung down into the battery

where cannons were stored.
In one photo of WWI, a practice drill,
men hold their ears as the cannon
goes off. In another, officers
form a makeshift band—
trumpets and French horns,
the piano behind, its bench empty.
A player piano? Who knows how long
between the death-prick and the death,
or how Rilke handled suffering
since his soul suffered so upon being born.
What angel hovered beside him
when they put the leeches on him?
What was her name? Her province—
comfort or pain? I used to think
his verses precious, but that might
have been just a bad translation.
How does it happen that a man
named for a woman, a man who writes
elegies and sonnets that foretell nature's
dominion over man, can suicide
of having been infected by a rose?
His was this other, made-up garden
of Orpheus and Eurydice—half-gods
who nourished him until he died
from the injection of pure beauty.

from The White Cypress

The Skull

You walked up Tabletop Mountain
And found a skull. A coyote, dog,
Or wolf—you are not sure.

Perhaps a deer. You run
Your finger along the teeth:
Yellowed ivories glowing,

Molars' compacted surfaces.
Not a single one missing—the animal
Died young. For the skeletal grin

You feel wistful, even as a man.
Is there a secret you missed
Along the way, a better kind of life

Lived among the ruins of nature
Rather than this entrapment
Where you fight your way through

Each urban day, return to the well-kept
House at night? You walked up Tabletop,
Looked far out where the shape-shifting

Begins again between brother
And sister mountains twisting
Sharp peaks southwest,

Blued by the moon raising its single horn
In the east. When you picked up
The skull it walked with you, breathed

Through eye sockets wide open
As with the sudden shocked surprise of—
You are not sure which—

Being dead or carried in you hand.

Washington Harbor

Lies inland,
like Prometheus' water-colored liver
dripping endearments, this daemon
full of salts, this frieze of abalone.

     Spit of land
where Frank lived in a duck shack.
Promontory where a shelf drops off into frigid water,
the trout you caught as a kid takes the bait,
runs out the line again until it breaks.

     As we separate
from one another, so salt water
waits upon the moon. As we live several
lives within a single lifetime, the fetus
embodies reptile, avian, human.

     The big house
sits high above, cliffside. Below,
burial grounds where a ring of shells
make bold the gulls who fling their oysters
on the rocks to break out yellow flesh.

Inland sea,
shallow lake, pond where herons open
like kites and fly toward the cliffs. Enclosed
not with coral, but twin culverts housed
beneath a road of sand.

Don't pretend
you can leave this lagoon—*lacuna*—
that you never wanted to lie down and feel sun
warm your legs young again, back propped
against half-whitened logs of driftwood
carried in during the last storm and left for dead.

Lagoon of longing,
where the pull of full moon plunged your belly
into cramps over what would not be born
or miscarried. Near Protection Island,
peacocks displayed mating rituals
for a twenty-something man and woman.

Lagoon sans dunes,
here sand's pebbled with star-colored stones.
Age tightens the circle—high tide bound to low.

Age favors—no, flatters—youth's warped memory.
Narcissus walked here, hurt these fragile plants,
too young to love anyone but himself.

Sin

after Franz von Stuck, *Sin*, 1906

Oh she is deadly, with the snake
twisted around her neck
and torso, with the frame
about her—a Roman pillar
on either side of her dark hair.

She isn't the kind of woman
you'd want your daughter
to be. Self-aggrandizement, fur,
a separate apartment for the snake—
she isn't anything

you would want for yourself.
Still, you can't help looking.
After all, she's housed in a museum.
The artist is more famous than anyone
post-modernity will remember.

Her nipples rise and touch the fabric—
fur, that is, of a garment
displaced by her breasts.
Her eyes, outlined in kohl, tell nothing
more than whatever wrestled her

from bed for the sake of portraiture.
Captured? Hardly. Confessed?
To no one but the snake
beside her mouth, that co-conspirator
who knows her inside out

as no man or woman can,
ever since the dirt floor held the imprint
of her foot. She stands there stirring
the dream you dreamt before you
were overcome by daylight.

Ants

They show up first in the kitchen.
Sugar ants—benign, gray as dust
on a dying man's eyelashes.
Next come slightly larger bodies,
segmented—these you recognize

from childhood, the small wings
like red flags: propagation.
Soon comes the army:
carpenter ants marching
their rows and columns

across the bed, infecting the house
with a contagion bred of neglect.
Outside boughs of cedar take over
the lilac, and rust-colored plants
grow into trees overnight.

When did your health go south?
Why does every meal taste the same?
How did your husband
find that other woman
in his office, and begin courting her

as if you hadn't mothered his children,
folded back his sheets, said little words
that passed for vows before the relatives.
The modest house goes back to nature.
Inertia breeds sickness,

Mold grows its lichens.
The temperature falls
as it does on the mountain.
Lowlands give way to higher ground
in the province of monstrosities,

where the stunted
masquerade as gnome, troll, goblin,
and, last of all, the elfin, waiflike,
fragile girl he once called *darling,*
honey, sweetheart.

Afterword

After the act—prima facie,
of his drowning by conceit—
came the floating. Head to sky,

his pupils empty
as a Roman statesman in that summer's
thunderhead-layered heaven.

Came autumn, its telltale
mole-mounds, dead possums,

raccoons hounded by Indian summer

searching garbage bins
with their all-too-human hands.
Trees around the property

put down roots for Narcissus
equal in length and breadth
to his longing for himself.

Their branches circling. Concentric
ripples sent from the stone of his head
into the water to speak in whispers

about the doppelganger lives
of lover and loved, adoring and adored.
Dead weight: the shroud,

the forest with its filial canopy.
The son of a patriarch, tongue-flowered
with light. How close the self

to its band of thought-accomplices.
How veer away from the proscriptive drama
of nature masquerading as myth

and archetype? Come the thick man,
a corpse for a copse. Come the horse in blinders
to witness everyman's Achilles' heel.

The Double Looney

It comes, Mother, complete
with a solid gold center.
Lifted from Canada,
dumb-thumbed, it comes
from your all-girl school
in the ghetto-lands.

Like the wind sweeping trees
of yellow leaves
in a Pacific storm, it's
sworn to secrecy, weighs
almost nothing, doesn't tell
its worth to strangers.

The black birds above the sky
could be leaves or coins,
the gusts swollen with water,
the mail truck passing,
flashing lights in early darkness.
Certain signals malinger

in the discs between my spine.
I call these pain for the way
they enter the hip
and the leg and refuse
to emigrate. I know at the border
you paused for a look

at Niagara Falls.
Would pocket change

hold up in the new land?
Would father finish his degree,
leave his den, enter the silence
of numbers sent to earth

from the sun? Would there be
children, and children's children?
This coin fits your sunny disposition,
and the way, drunk after a bottle
of red wine—any kind will do—
your laughter brightens, its

tinned edge—is tin an element
in the periodic table? I know
salt follows us wherever we go,
onions bring tears, a bit of oil
sizzling in the pan recalls
your ample breasts and full-

figured spirit. What I didn't know
then I know now—you were
not really a saint, rather crazed
with the same anxieties that rule
my days. Mother, the original
loony, called to be less than,

equal to, more than, the task
at hand—I have underestimated
your wealth. This gift—take it
while you limp among the living,
your balance gone, left ear
deaf to the sinister ones.

Their whispers, as always,
escaped your sense of smell
which was, as you said,
bad to nil, though you cooked
our feasts. In them we tasted
your tongue and heart.

In the slivers of spice from Provence
or Montreal that greened
the fish we proclaimed the meal
good, we took to your kitchen
table the shadow lands of our need
for nurture, for relief from hunger

and pain. Mother,
though we never equated
our suffering with your pocketbook
we took all you offered
us as subsidy, we left you
with less than a silver dollar.

Infanticide

After you suffocate the baby
you go searching
through cabinets for cereal,
unnerved by its blue body, its fat cheeks
white under the viselike grip.

After you suffocate the baby
you hear strangers talking outside.
You wonder whether the wind
has borne witness to this dream act,
the most honest.

There were avenues to travel, certain
details open to interpretation.
What puzzles you most—the guilelessness
of the eight or nine-month old,
how it went along with the plot,

putting its mouth in your hand.
nuzzling your fingers like a mutt.
On the night you suffocate the infant—
you who never remember your dreams—
the clarity of baby, hand, bassinette

refuses to leave its place
beside other known quantities:
water, the spit of land blown clean
save for black and white
sand that rushes into clothing

with a vengeance, like carpenter ants
burrowing into a stump
for the sake of the colony,
or the hole in your cheek—
that double.

Epstein Barr

At the bottom
            of the tea cup,
the last leaves of lemon grass
spell a new fortune:
            There will be a nap in your future.

That future has already
become
          a past. Each day's worth
of tea-leavings:
                    a bog
from which my tired body,
mired
          hip-to-shoulder—
          tries to slog its slow way
                    way up from.

In the kitchen, the bright
          clatter of cutlery. And
the high-pitched chatter,
                              the laughter
of relatives
          I'm named after.
Their sharpened knives
          chop chives on the oiled
block. Heady scents
rise from
          wooden scars.

It will be gradual,
the return to health—
          tendered by the same
                              hidden hands
that furrow my brow,
give me my
          upside-down smile.

I am the joke
          my family of strangers visits.
I am their laughter

and sigh,
their catharsis at not being me
       palpable
as a lemon
              stung by its second cut.

Box Turtle

We found a turtle beside the trail.
An oar had gouged its shell,
such a deep wound, you said,
and look how it has healed.

You took the turtle and carried it carefully
as a glass creature towards
the lake. Hid the turtle in rushes close to water.
We knew the end of the story,

how a lonesome boy, stumbling
through underbrush, would find
the turtle and take it home. He'd
put it in a box and keep it under his bed,

until his mother put an end to things.
We found the turtle beside a trail
in a public park. Who knows what blade
left the gash that remains upon us

like a wound, as if it were we
who were marked by the violence
of pleasure and leisure,
we who had to bear the insolence

of not knowing whether or when
the burial took place,
what kind of ritual accompanied it,
and was there a makeshift cross,

the boy already learning
what it meant to be a man
as he knit two sticks together
with a vine of nightshade.

My Penance

Flowers at dusk
against black trees.
I pay as one
who digs holes
for dahlia-tubers,
kneeling beside newly turned
rows close
to darkness. Holding
brown fists to my chest.
My penance
is like the staid
gray settler horse
who walks thoroughbreds
on their rounds
from stall to stall
at the race. Like
lit signals, roads,
and houses
across the lake.
It is a harbor where
the log drifts

like a seal pup
left to drown at low
tide. I give back useless
stems, wild cherries,
petals storm-tossed,
daubed on just-cleaned
windows. Or, then
again, the full
bleeding moon set
low and orange
westward, and south.

October

And the wild rose
blooms again in stillness before rain.
October, song of my sister, of the psalms
said for gratitude against the coming

of sickness and gray days—one long day
lasts the whole of winter, one long night
that never lightens.
The wild rose strains to birth

one more blossom, to tinge the edge
of winter's sword with blood.
We who live in houses—
the lucky ones, we see and do not understand

men who sleep beneath bridges,
their heads cradled in cardboard boxes.
We know the tides come and go
as sickness comes and goes.

Our neighbor's bones will break and mend,
our children's children will fall
and be well. October, and the wild rose
raises itself up

at once plain and pretty
as if to right every wrong
done to the kingdom of ants and bees—
all those who live communally.

A Tattooed Lady

If she wanted to be seen
she would not have emblazoned
her breasts with irises,
and vines that reached
heart-shaped up her sternum
and, from there to her collarbone
where they became another flower
with long stamens and cups
butterflies could drink from.

If she wanted to be seen
she would not have Polynesia
permanent as a country on one thigh,
her shin embellished
by a military island, small,
bounded by blue waters.

The needle would puncture her skin
like a wasp, leaving the sting
that couldn't kill what it stung.
The inks would be inserted like desire—
indelible, exotic.

If she wanted to be seen
she would not have brought
the turtleneck sweater to wear later.
Rap beat its own tattoo in the back room
where alcohol and peroxide
blended like a martini she loved too much
to drink.

In order not to be seen
she would have to love the pain—
it marked her as alive.
She cried like a sandpiper.
Her back filled with peacocks,
their blistered feather-eyes
iridescent as morphine.

If she wanted to be seen
she wouldn't have an insignia, *tau*,
nineteenth letter of the Greek alphabet,
etched above her ankle.
This toos could be read as a cross.
It might mean forever to a lover.

If she wanted to be seen,
lying naked in the motel that stank
of cigarettes and air freshener,
her head pillowed on sheets
rough and lemony as a hair shirt,
she would not have pulled the string
attached to a bulb that went dark.

June Bug

Heat dozes in the road.
You think of your father,
his love for the stars,
those summer evenings

he'd sit with a newspaper
on a chair in the back yard.
Clearing his throat repeatedly
as if to speak.

You know about the beetle—
its sly reprisal, snuggled
to a fig branch. A fig eater.
Analysis could be that simple.

You eye its injured wing.
Like a prop plane
at the end of the driveway,
pulled from midair by the cat.

Upon its back a scarab
shines emerald in early August dark.
The plums have begun
to rot, the blueberries go green

to purple fewer and farther between.
As for mother—you have
already become her, taken on
her middle as well as her age.

You recognize in the emerald
a birthstone, the need
for odd or even—54
or 7. Prime numbers

or easily divisible.
You carry forward father's
shattered nerves. Startle easily,
follow the same book—

avoid the tests. Yes.
Best to stick with what myopia
understands: that the kill
has already taken place.

The White Cypress

> "Behind the cypress curtain…"
> Nabokov

Those who fatten
On the dead—they're
     Never far from us, those
Others
We worship, the ones who received rough treatment at our hands
    When they were alive
        And gave us our lives…

*

Those who contend with the terror-laden place
    Called purgatory, placed here, on earth
     Where the tree, while bearing up
Under flowers,
Cannot be cut down—

The freeway a clot beside which a bit of green
Contains the last nest
      Of marbled mullet, mother and chicks.

Where the tree lives longer than the human
      And is engaged with infertility
A drama occurs
Between a man and a woman.

The child
Who refuses conception
      As if it were a sordid engagement—
Who can lay blame?

*

Old bark signatures
Mimicked by Durer
By Dali
By the Catalonian landscape
      Where Gaia becomes a praying mantis.

Oedipus leaves the usual stony ruins.
Narcissus probes the skin of water with his mouth, his nose, his
      lungs…

*

Vis a vis a ribbon
      Hung from a branch
Beside THE OLD HOUSE UNDER THE CYPRESS TREE

In which Stalin gave the Russians hell on earth
      The Caucasus rose domed with snow
      As Zhivago went to die with Tanya

                    His writing desk consonant
With winter.

*

Those who fatten themselves
On the dead—
Let them have their elegies, forms and stories
            To regale the ones
They scorned in life.

*

The same three fates
Hold a length of thread.
It's they who spin our life span still—
            Who measure, cut, twist
            The double image: a doppelganger
                    Composed of dream and myth.

The Blackberry Hedge in Autumn

Here the birds come to twitter
about what's left after the harvest moon
grows orange and swollen, so heavy
it finally falls from the sky.

I hear your argument again.
You'll be the slow suicide,
eat yourself to death with sugar.
No better way to go,

the birds say, with a sound
that plays like joy on a day so dank
it's good it will end early, finish
with a glimpse of sun yellow as the last plum tomato

left to ripen inside a tire rim.
It's a thick thing to be left behind,
the birds sing. *Better late than never.*
I hear their platitudes

blend with chimes someone has set
outside a window
to catch breezes off the lake.
Whatever metal's left in me

has gone soft. Here the birds
lose a major scale
and find it plaited to the minors.
There's nothing left to resolve, only

the laggard pace of fall, stale leaves
rotting in a ditch.
Poplar, birch, oak, cherry.
What difference does it make?

The songbird orchestra tunes,
checks one reed against another,
ostracizes a gull the color of lake water.
One more pedestrian idea gone to seed.

That I could save you from
your own appetites?
The blackberries picked over, shrunken,
bitter, too far gone to matter.

Lemon

At this time in the morning
it's a truck
carrying the sun.

Late afternoon it stains the avocado
a woody green.
It carries synesthesia,

the taste we want to hear.
It holds the privacy of the inner sectors,
fine and lustrous.

The cartel's gone quiet
except for one robin
who bears the blood of the world.

At this time of evening
there is only the lemon
and its clone.

Twin lemons:
one to be sacrificed,
the other exalted.

Yellow doubled in the lemon.
Lemon yoked like an egg
to a cloak of slumber.

Lemon of mourning,
hounding our dreams
with its bright-bitter taste.

The tiger pauses in lemongrass
before pulling
its prey into the baobab tree.

Lemon swathed in thick skin,
bound to the graves of earth
by wooden shafts of light.

Becalmed

The cherry in flower,
the children gone,
the lust for lust
grown into a different creature,
one who sits in a patch of sun.

The sky-ships
welded together like clouds
nibbled at the edge
by portraiture's downy curls
and the blue gaze of youth.

A willow gestures, hemmed
by the same kite strings
that bind a woman to the hours.
Her figure changed by what
she cannot resist—

that pear listing
on the sill, this apple pressed
against another apple
in a crystal bowl.
Whatever the wind possessed,

it released to wander
over these lands changed
from exotic to familiar,
a sleight of hand
turning courtyard to yard,

the fountain at the center
of the square holding nymphs
and cherubs above water
as if both were innocent.
The cherry squanders its beauty

in bursts, ousts its scent
like a provocateur—
coyness overflowing the bowl
where child and woman
lived for years under the same roof.

Tribal Moon Cycle

Hard Moon

Cold moon, goose moon.
The sun has not strength to thaw.
      Barren,
bear-hunting moon.
Wolves run together.

Hard moon, goose moon,
cold moon—the year is not done.
      Another age
in her winter houses,
it will be new again.

This wind comes to our old ones
sharp as an arrowhead.
      We listen for wolves.
We sleep on a crust of dreams—
one eye closed, one eye open.

This is her coldest moon.
We hunt, wait for coyote
      to come, ice to melt.
For the budding moon of plants
and shrubs, a shred of green.

Coyote Moon

Bony moon.
Moon when the trees crack,
drop ice-dead boughs.

We stand shoulder to shoulder
around the fire moon.

This is black bear moon.
Ice in the river is gone.

We sleep in a ring
to keep the yellow hunger
from stealing our young.

Catching-Fish Moon

Warming moon, moon
        of the sore eyes.

Day moon, noisy goose moon—
        see the *V* fly.

Unwieldy birds cross broad waters lapping
        scalloped edges.

Doves come in pairs to firs—
        coo coo cooing.

Seagulls' bibbed iridescence flocks the willow's
        green-blanched kite strings.

Even the thick-toed dancers
        grow pretty in time.

We no longer stand shoulder to shoulder
        around the fire moon.

Our toll paid in full, we walk lightly beneath
    arching branches.

Melting Moon

Red grass appears
beneath a thin-rimmed crescent.

A duck decorates a pot,
and the man who dips his ladle
finds food which grows upon the water:

Nanaboozhoo returned from hunting...
As he came towards his fire, there was a duck
sitting on the edge of his kettle of boiling water.

After the duck flew away, Nanaboozhoo
looked into the kettle and found wild rice
floating upon the water...

When the eighth moon comes the wife
cracks bones for marrow fat. She sets corn.

If there are no deer, geese fly past,
honking low across the lake.
Flowers grow from scratch.

Listen, long grains of rice
are flowing upward, tan
as the moon dangling above the plain.

This is the time when
the air buds, and mud hens
rest upon the water.

Moon When the Ponies Shed

Lilacs. Moon before pregnancy,
when the women weed corn.

With budding breasts, I walked among men
who were hungry for my flesh.

Born in this month, I had no knowledge
of the uses my body could be put to.

I only wanted to brush and curry the fur
of my fourteen-hand high horse.

To clean his frogs, pulling the stones
from his hooves, which he lifted

at the touch of my hand, and placed back down
on the ground for me alone.

Summer Starting

Strawberry Moon,
red-flower moon.

Birth Moon,
moon of pain.

Moon when we hill the corn,
our backs to the sun.

9th Moon,
unborn head crowding belly.

Moon when the berries turn purple-black,
indigo.

In our planting of Moons
we become a place.

Green silk leafed Moon,
sky turquoise as after rain.

Long-Days Moon
to lighten these short nights.

Beneath branches of Milky Way
live the widening night Sequoias.

Red Blooming Lilies

Fish spoils easily
as we go about
the work of women
and children—collection.

Ripe corn moon.
Bending down,
each kernel glistens
like petals of a flower.

Squash ripen
near blackberry patches.
Like bees hovering
close to a flower,

we have honeyed uses
for fish, corn, and squash.
We know many ways
to scale, shell, peel.

How many days left
to pick, taste, spit out pits
before the cherries,
the chokeberries, go black?

Drying up Moon

Summer. Heat
takes the water
from our mouths,
and gives us thirst.

We use cedar bark
for hats and baskets.
Moon of the ripening—
all things must swell

and burst, or else
they dry and shrivel.
There is no choice
when sun bakes soil.

Cracks trace patterns
in dirt. Whether we gaze
straight ahead, up, or down,
we see only yellow.

Big Moon

Calves grow hair.
This is her acorns' moon,
her ice moon—
moon of the dry leaves.

The chill takes sun
lower each night.
We say *kálk kungáay*.
Frost rings our breath.

We live in huts
built with our hands.
Our work begins again,
sound and light enough

to hold the cold,
the young, the old ones,
and those in between,
beneath the circle.

Moon When the Wind Shakes off Leaves

This is travel in canoes moon.
We paddle across waves
deep in the trough,
white at the crest.
Young animals moon.
Rutting.
Changing seasons.
In the middle,
between harvest
and eating corn.
We put away provisions.
We are lucky
to have the ill-smelling
sticky fish. To wear fur
taken off the carcass
of rabbit and bear
around our faces.

Trading Moon

Scraping moon.
Scraping by moon.
Snowy mountains in the morning,
we go to barter
this for that.
Without our brothers
we would not have oil.
We would not have nutmeats
and preserved berries.

Without the others
we would be frail,
falling leaves,
skinned, unable
to hibernate
when winter begins.

When Deer Shed Their Antlers

Now unborn seals
are getting hair
inside their mothers.

Against the hills the deer
shed their horns, heads too heavy
to carry any longer
on jut-ribbed bodies.

Much white frost on grass.
How long before
her winter houses' moon
gives way to the other season?

How many more days
do we go walking without
good food? Without light?

How slowly the snow moon
ebbs and flows, low down
in the sky, bearing the news
of dark: more darkness.

New Poems

Closed Head Injury

I don't remember what happened
                        before,
except, as I lay on my back
on the asphalt,
I dreamt I was still shopping
                        for a raincoat
            for my husband.

I'd carried my two-year old past
a donut shop, where
policemen sat beneath
            garish lights.

How it troubled me, to hear
that woman
            screaming the name
                        of her son.

The doctors say I was lucky.
The accident: a hit and run.

And now time drifts
            and I float on it
like a paper boat
                        down a storm sewer.

More than likely,
nothing preceding
            the five minutes before
the five minutes before
                        an ambulance siren
can ever be erased from the brain's
gray matter,
            its cache and sieve.

And I, almost happy—
as if listening to
           wind-fed
      rapids
rushing down rock faces—
             foam frothing,
                swollen.

The Phoenix

for T.

Because it was called *fire bird*
you went looking for it at night
in dangerous cities.

Because of its five-hundred year life span
you felt compelled to stamina.
And because, in every ancient culture—

Persian, Greek, Arabic, Chinese, Roman—
the creature made the same nest,
you thought you'd find a fantastical oak

in Berlin, spreading fat branches
over widows who walked slowly
with their cloth shopping bags

beneath street lamps placed at intervals
along the Avenue of Lindens.
Instead you took a tram, met others

who, unlike yourself, had found speck of gold
clinging to the soles of their shoes,
and, soon enough, became the place they chose to dig in.

Still, the red beak troubled you.
Was Ovid right? Not to eat fruit and flowers,
rather to prefer to feast on gums?

You knew about strong will—
how men long to break, most of all,
those who possess a homeland and a song.

Those who would, when their alarm
went off, travel to Egypt to bury
the father who taught them lessons.

You knew once it built that nest nothing
and no one could stop
the immolation.

And, because you did not feel not safe
near a myth of such proportions,
you took to calling yourself *pagan*.

Anger

Each time I wash
them my sheets soften,
so I wash them
every day. Once
the world was like this—
white, shining, its gleam
like the sun behind
my eyes, an afterimage
on a bright morning.
I take towels
down to the river

and pound them to hear
the sound of fists.
I rinse my fear
in the mouths
of crocodiles, carry
the weight of water
on my head.
Clay jars spill,
soak into my spine's
mud-brown circles,
compressed now
like the earth
of the broad path
others walk. Always
to the same canal
full of minnows,
a stream wedded
to runoff, named
for its own mountain.

Aegis

After she lost her shield, Athene
turned toward the hills. Not sure
whether to come or go, no longer
bound by Zeus or Apollo.
After she lost her child nothing
came between her lap and the other
women, temptresses who
would take what she'd found
of safety. Finally alone,
the hard questions came. Was
her father the first?

Or Zeus? Migraines took food
from her stomach. Auras came
into her mind, stayed on
like afterimages of the sun.
One day she shut herself
in. A room with stone windows,
a chink of light, sounds of waves
and birds. Would no one pass
her story on? Those strangers
who came upon her leather
body, the wineskin long
empty, the dates shrunk to raisins?
Without a shepherd, even goats
wander off from the yard
of a house shaded by blackberries.

My Father Returns as the Jack in the Box in a Dream

He's waited on the bed to spring up at me, always
the same clay face, skin the color of flesh.
Of course, in the silence that ensues, you'll have
to take my word for this. As when one tells a dream
it disappears—but no, my father, a little figure—
still attached to the tiny bed from which he leaps
like a rattler coiled in the heat. Like a monster
to scare schoolgirls, and this would happen every
time I opened the door, as dreams are not past, present
nor future. When I was eighty years old my father
was still made of dough, under-baked, yeasty, never risen
quite enough to believe in…when I was seventy
my father sprung from the box and the phrase he said,
well you'll have to content yourself, I don't remember.

Jacob's Ladder

I see several plants in astigmatism—
points of phlox and star.
I have phobias of height and closed-in places.

There will be no reprieve for my mother,
the bearded woman,
and none for my father,

who wore a bell-shaped petal on his sleeve.
He was only counting to supplant
his older brother, Jake. His numbers,

infinitesimally small, return each August
as Jacob's Ladder draws in
its browns, whispers like chimes

whose music has its own way of dying—
pulling back, pining for dominance, or closure.
The burning bush turns bright

even if red is due to drought.
Each autumn brings its own peculiar
complications. No asphodel

will be left alive,
no father seized by the heel,
determined to sacrifice his son as proof of loyalty.

Only the elements remain—iron, sulphur, tin.
Slightly blued under the alchemy of dawn,
the last radicals left on earth.

Leaves gone wooden,
they steel themselves for another climb
away from and toward.

Montreal, 1946

My mother passes Jackie Robinson
on the street. She's just fifteen, realizes
only after he passes—Jackie
Robinson! This is back when he was
in the farm leagues, taken away from
the United States. When the law of
segregation ruled even in the field.

My mother passes Jackie, looks back,
yells *Hi!* Robinson doesn't hear.
He's tall and lean, a stand-out. Melting
snow in curls around curbs, a northern Spring.

Mother's father takes her to games when
her brother's occupied with other
things. That's how she recognizes the man
who will be king. Her story comes with red
wine, half a bottle left, the aftermath
of dinner with family. Four generations.

Who can say why this story, held closer
than the others we know by heart by now,
had to wait so long? Who can say Jackie
Robinson didn't hear her yell, and,
already cocksure in his new home
away from home, decided not to turn,
not to look back at the adolescent
girl fawning in her threadbare coat.

Cause and Effect

If I wind up my hand
it will play a song. No, listen,
if I get down on my knees
and beg, if underneath the ferns
there are insects with voices,
some big-celled argument
comes true. Behind the grimace
in cold spring the word *romance*,
if I wind up my hand.
A certain cruelty thrives.
Beneath the forest floor spongy
with mushroom-laced spoors.
After the canopy of the trees
beings with extra shadows
copy themselves onto trunks
and water. The comb holds
our sex, and the pattern of violence
makes and mocks us.
If I wind up my hand
it will play the tune
you wanted to hear.

In the Black Forest

As in a German fairy tale,
the trees dark
and widely spaced,
the forest floor well-swept

by a cretin.
Near the Avenue of Lindens,
close to a Holocaust memorial,
we walked.

The Spree, a ribbon of silver
ground down each day by hulls and sails,
this river proved, by tint and shade,
that water was a foil

and land a grave.
Each day cranes made the city
well or ill. Trams drained people
from stations and filled them up again.

Museums and churches
were fertile grounds for thought,
but not the forest. There
I wore my Gabardine and still was cold.

How much do you remember?
Each tree held a plaque with a number.
We joked about the Germans,
their need for order.

No underbrush.
The cretin kept well out of view,
his broom always poised at the threshold
of the next fork in the story.

We posed in monotone.
What was left of our intimacy
followed, like bread crumbs,
the path that led to a prison.

There we dreamt we were well fed,
that what we kept back from one another
couldn't be told apart
from what we surrendered.

Thirteen

Not the moon's perpetual adolescence,
its white gasoline issuing from behind
the maple, as open-windowed cars play
rap songs rude as midnight. Not the many-
storied decrepitude within which

a dolphin-shaped pawn's taken away from
the board. Rather chlorine, salt, radio—
back when there were stations and DJ's
who chorused time to turn before you burn—
the bikini-line you saw, when, stripped

and ready for anything, nothing happened.
Not this residual full-moon feeling,
the party going on without you, the blacklight
pulsing with fluorescence against
Elvis posters. Not the urgency, fluid

now, masked by nothing redder than lipstick
and anger, lipstick and thick-lashed lids—lip
and more lip until the train's come and gone
with the same whoosh the moon would make, only
whiter. You think your rage will end that way—

in a tunnel. Mole-blind, hours later,
after they dare you to down paper cups
of Scotch. Forget about single, double—
you don't yet know how to gauge what's good.
Shell-pink palate sugared, overloaded

with sodas and sweets. Still less you know
how anything gets privilege, left inside
a barrel or the trunk of a car. If
gender's a popsicle, age—well, age might
as well be a pickle, or malt sprinkled

like snow over ice cream at Willie's,
where photographs leer from crooked walls:
the largest banana split in history
shot in black and white. Skinny-tied men ogling
the girl who pops out of a layer cake.

Shingles

My body,
   their house.
Their raised welts,
      the overlapping siding.

As if a carpenter
         living inside my hip
works ceaselessly,
   digging at synapses with his awl.

I am driven
      in the fallen world
by whorls

that tell me where
my nerves lie.

Once-pale skin
reddens, thickens,
 seeps yellow fluid.
Sealing my joints,
  their blistered hinges.

Devil's itch
   that festers
at questions
 beyond good, evil.

Shall we be bitter
   or resigned,
the burnt skin
plucked at, as pain's
 lyre, singing
at dawn?

Such a Long Life

In memory of Jack Gilbert

At first it is the salt-taste of bridges,
the strangeness of animals,
the orange horizon scrawled
by winter sunset. We take this lineage in,
and it gives us back our own, like Bluebloods
persecuted in a forest. We come to be afraid
of limned windows, the strangers
behind blinds, the streetlights haloed
by myopia, the past pulling all our fathers
into hunger's single crib. The more we stare

at the moon, the more we see its pockmarks
and pits, seas and valleys where once
the surface was undisturbed. In this
we are like the children we bear,
who give back their immortality
as if it were nothing more than a coin
to be thrown in a well after the one wish was made.
With little more than half a moon
and the rain-gnawed spit-misted sun,
we come of age in order to bear luster,
to beat our short arms
against the swath of blue-green that hovers
in the brevity between.

The Sifting

Through the long hours of afternoon,
the torture of opera wedded to scents
of rising bread, a river of cardamom
merging with poppy seeds—this was the art
of childhood, not to be mastered, rather,
conquered by. All through the long hours
of an afternoon punctuated
by swipes of viola bow and their
attendant flats, always in residence
in the house of my parents, humbled
but not poor, its windows tinted by rain
sun, or snow, a house immoderately
fond of its yard, a yard gone spindly
with saplings in whose arches ballerinas
twirled, jeted, and pirouetted come evening,
when droplets, flakes, or hail from Thor
fell, and thunder.

Wind

Like pain it came and left by halves
and now mostly it stays on,
a boarder too poor to leave.

Like cottonwood it coated scenes
of past lives, and now it breathes in
heady gusts of her, as chunks calve

from her ego the way a glacier loosens
its sides to water. Wind, like air,
is not like anything, she thinks.

Ivory sheers hang to blot
the sun's bright face close to solstice.
She didn't think she'd end up like this,

one of Macbeth's three witches
stirring words together, whispering
curses under her breath

like her father. All tenses conspire.
Sun lights hearts of ivy, the yard
overgrown, as when desire

first departed on its thin-ribbed horse
for another land, and the door
slammed shut of its own accord.

Wolf Spider

It comes with the smell of water in the desert
of summer. August, and everything rust-colored.
It is only a myth told by the grown-ups to scare you
into eating a dish too rich for your flat stomach.
Then again, how quickly the arachnid disappears
beneath the siding of your childhood house.
As if it knew you meant some kind of harm. You'd set
an opaque vase over it while screaming curses.
You'd hide the over-done despotic fur legs.
Just the edge of this phobia makes the skin on your forearm
crawl. You would claw your scalp until it bled
to remove the demon that nests in your just-washed hair.

House of Burnt Cherry

after "Paris in Winter," by William Logan

Here the martyr and the porcupine
live together, for here they both belong.
Cross the foyer, see two huddled shapes
planted on the sofa ages ago,
bled of light. Come from the Old World,

the spine hog and the one who suffers
torture. Long after midnight the trough
of desire—dry-needled, rotten—leaves
its bee sting on Saint Sebastian.
Here wallpaper peels back the psalms. Scents

of musk rise from stained upholstery.
A rodent's stiff, coarse hairs line the martyr's
back, interspersed with red markings,
where sharp quills dug in pretty zzz's
of memory and sleep. Dreams he never

forgets, incidents inscribed on skin.
Beams laid log-cabin style: an outpost
avoided by mailman and assassin,
milkmaid, fannier, and village idiot.
No wonder they hardly get along—

two hogs snuffling at sills to find a bit
of seed. Two states underscored by need.
Two almost-persons married to pity's
cousin, guilt. Like twins who nestle
in the womb, they take up whatever room

yields. Fetal position, hands covering ears.
Oxygen finds a way to enter.
Wasn't the umbilical a channel,
the stink of wood freshened by a blade,
the moon put out by its own candled-wound.

My Grandmother's Waltz

One breast gone, soft arms doughy, arms extended,
no longer a woman, rather a specter,
she danced in torn slippers, her hair short-cropped.

One two three, one two three. And we, *die kinder,*
were of one mind in our jury as children:
we had, in our infinite power

made her into a kind of a contraption—
a Babushka spinning in its own squat body.
Always the counting beneath whistles of trains

running westward from the town of no money.
Always the wheeze of a breathy laughter
following its own spittle around the rheumy

house, which was half of a house. In the foyer
she blessed us with three quick spits on our heads.
Large flowers splattered a shift held together

with safety pins. Wooden floors she twirled
were scarred with nails. How could she be happy?
We made her smile, late afternoons, doilies seeded,

yellowed with age. The sun crept away,
the last train left as Bartok began again,
piano baring monstrous teeth. *One two three,*

one two three, one arm wound around my brother,
the other held out to me, she danced
to her own songs—accompanied gutturals.

So what if Poland wept for her blued
eyes, the cataract of mountains rearranging
what was once home before the flatlands.

Had we concocted this underling?
What could we do to send her back upstairs
to the room of garments, mothballed, hanging.

There, a hundred netted hats waited for her.
Like persons with no faces their tongues swished
five languages inside-out together

as she read Agatha Christies in Polish,
pausing only to extract a piece of green
from the thin mouth unlipsticked, sheepish

almost in its shy smile as another roast burned
in the oven, and we went free to giggle
and climb in her orchard. There, apples, stunted

by fear of heights, would give a little
sour from their crabs, thrill the sky with danger,
make unleavened earth eat its own gristle.

Notes for the Defense

Before it spun out of control,
red beak pitched downward,
before it went off like a firecracker

*

decoupage-crazed indigo and alizarin,
omen-draped, dove-tailed,
riding thermals into the pyre—
before it had lived long enough
to become sick of life

*

we thought it would have taken more to bring it down.
What about
its helium ego, the pinprick
in the balloon, yada yada…

*

For all the accolades heaped upon its meager head
it appeared to have the same cheek
as Ovid did when corrected.

*

What rotten baggage foisted by scholars:
the gum and frankincense, cinnamon and myrrh,
some parallels airstrips running along
the narrow strip of land called *agrarian*.
What of the religious foment? Dismiss as mere
ledge between communal dream
and three wise men.

*

How become blue-blood, rose-madder,
gobbled by the fire
instinct started?

*

Would there be yet another replicate,
a phoenix
rising from the ashes
as if to bring some Pollyanna chit
to the nakedness of life, the maladroit, those possessed
by nerve pain?

*

Had anyone ever thought whether the bird's
fastidious maleness
prevented there being an egg?

*

Where there is no egg,
no conception. The philosophers smoked cigarettes—
smoke blued the image of the stale bird
housed in lecterns, museums, and story.

*

What of the journey to Egypt,
where it purportedly goes on schedule
once every five hundred years
to bury its already dead father

*

in the joke of a fire
started with spices?

*

Consider immolation,
cessation, the gestation
of mimetic birds

*

as brief sparks
come wafting through
French doors. Or fragments
from the ever-widening pyre, both womb and tomb,
begetting and devouring:

*

imagination.

Naugahyde

Skin of the animal called *Nauga*,
upon whose back we sat in cars,
on sofas and chairs, their history
carved into yellow linoleum floors,
gored into gray hardwoods.

As we struggled to attach,
the *Nauga* picked no favorites.
It held nothing but time, the shark's grin,
the webbed feet and stapled eyes
of a creature with vinyl skin.

We sat in its lap, oblivious to grown up
talk. Dust took to the air, covered
our featherweight, porcelain skins
until we, like the children
in Renaissance paintings,

became shamed by Mother's pots
banging around the kitchen, within range
of Father. The *Nauga* oozed sanction,
unlike those stuffed others
whose insides bled white fluff.

Held in flux. Bored,
fidgety, or slipping down
into scents of grease and lemon,
we'd eat dirt until its solicitous,
grimy repetitions became rituals

to summon sleep: a black and white TV,
an ironed woman smoking cigarettes
while running her vacuum
back and forth across a blinded house
on any given snowy afternoon.

High Strung

I weave the night
from nothing in particular:
a rebellion against, a trampling upon,
the instant before fight or flight.

Green blood in the culverts,
frogs high-jumping
from bank to medusa head—
an upended tree
slipped into the river by storm.
The end of days, where a man,
picnicking in a field fenced by poplars
loses his keys.

I am the metal detector
aimed at grass, the potato bug
curled like a fetus,
the slender branch erupting
from its swath of blackberries and thorns,
stripped, excited by wind.

I am the green horse, the insomniac.
Always the same lesson,
studied and lost like the man's keys,
or the young woman

on hands and knees searching
a hectare for its purse.

When the moon's just past full,
on the brink of autumn,
corn silk whispering
against leaves, I am the fist
and the money.

Go ahead, plant my feet.
The cliff falls away
when you run
with your orange wings,
with the man on your back.
All you see below the ledge
can be taken like a pulse.

Cloisonné

I like the swirl of colors, enameled,
inlaid, in leaves falling early,
the compartments of sky and water,
the rooftops neatly hammered into place
beyond news of an infant whose heart
murmur indicates something larger.

I like the gauze screens covering dirty
glass panes, through which I see floaters
rising and falling like silver wires
in my eyes. The geode slices perched
in the window glitter like gemstones,
their opaque centers lit by noon-light.

There is a voice behind the voice,
a light behind the light—even, perhaps,
some vitreous presence in the kiln
that sits on four legs like a lion,
inside the porch of memory.
There the temperature rises, and I remain

protected by the same thick walls
that protect me from bad news.
I like the sadness each harbor contains,
vessels bobbing with white triangles
cut from sailcloth. I think
I was outfitted in images, jewels

and clothes to catch something else
with my bowl, its nine colors
of enamel holding words, birds,
petals, snakes, ivy. Its suspicious
hearts wrought in blue and red, the lattice
edge finished with gold filigree.

Notes

Coppelia, Certain Digressions:
In "Bruxism," the expression "Et si male nunc, non olim sic ecrit," ("If things are bad now they will get worse") is a line altered from Horace, *Odes:* "If things are bad now, they will not remain that way" ("My Cousin's Corner Window, Hoffman.)

"Asafetida" is a German spice.

Regarding the character "Coppelia," the woman in Hoffman's tale substantially varies from the well known ballet, "Coppelia." The ending to the tale is dark; the ending to the ballet, lighter and more optimistic.

Madame de D. was a seven-year old girl, one of the first patients to be diagnosed in the early 1900's with Tourettes Syndrome by Dr. George Gilles de Tourette. The syndrome wasn't taken seriously until late in the 20th century.

"The Sunflower" was inspired by Goethe's "The Sorrows of Young Werther." The character of in Emma Zunz in the poem "Reprisal" appears in Jorge Luis Borges *Collected Fictions*, Penguin Press, 1998.

According to Greek myth, Procrustes was a host who adjusted his guests to fit their beds by lopping off ankles or placing their bodies on the rack. His name means "he who stretches." He kept a house by the side of the road, and offered his torturous hospitality to passing strangers.

*

Prisoner of the Swifts:
"Prisoner of the Swifts" is dedicated to Pamela Gross, with gratitude.
"*Nature Morte*" means "still life" in French, and is where the term originated.

In the poem "Breath Hunger," *chela* refers to the pincer of a crab or lobster.

"More Tenderly" was written for Jack Gilbert.

"The Seam" was written as part of an ongoing collaboration with textile artist Erika Carter.

*

The Never.
In the poem "The Death of Pan," the word *syrinx* refers to an archaic hand-made flute.

In "The Dodo Bird," lines quoted from Friedrich Hölderlin are taken from "Hymns," *Hymns and Fragments*, Princeton University Press, Princeton NJ © 1984.

The assertion by Céline in "The Rat" is taken from Louis-Ferdinand Céline, *North.* Translated by Ralph Manheim. Dalkey Archive Press, ©1996.

Quoted passages in "Extinction's Cousin" are taken from an essay by Ian Parker, *The New Yorker,* January 22, 2007.

*

The White Cypress.
The epigraph for "The White Cypress" is taken from Nabokov 's words in the essay "On Hodasevich," from *Shades of Love: Nabokov's Intimations of Immortality.* Ellen Pifer. The Kenyon Review. New Series, Vol. 11, No. 2 (Spring, 1989), pp. 75-86.

"The Double Looney" takes its inspiration from the Canadian two-dollar coin by the same name.

In the poem "Lemon," the word "synesthesia" refers to "a neurological condition in which stimulation of one sensory or cognitive pathway leads to automatic, involuntary experiences in a second sensory or cognitive path-way" *Wikipedia.*

The phrase "sky-ships" in "Becalmed" is borrowed from Herman Hesse. *Poems.* Translated by James Wright. Farrar, Straus and Giroux, New York. 1970.

*

"Tribal Moon Cycle" poems were written as part of a collaboration with visual artist Joan Stuart Ross. The intent of this series is to highlight the ways in which Native American, or first Nation tribes, lived in a state of wholeness with their environment. The fertility and abundance of moonlight is nowhere so revered as in the simple lexicon of the American Indian tradition of "naming" the moons for each month. A simple count of the number of names for one month may run to twenty different words and/or phrases. The Tribal year may begin with March or August; however, this information seemed too ambivalent to incorporate into the series. The month names have been removed, but the sequence begins with the Roman-Judeo calendar year: January. Tribes American Indian moons are taken from include: Algonquin, Cherokee, Lakota, Shawnee, Sioux, Tlingit, Wishram (WWU Planetarium, Encyclopedia Britannica Online).

Special thanks to Barbara L. Thomas, who assisted me in finding the "false notes" in earlier versions of this work. Ms. Thomas is eastern Cherokee. Her family escaped the Trail of Tears by hiding in the Smoky Mountains of Virginia.

*

New Poems:
I am grateful to Pamela Gross for her assistance with *Closed Head Injury* and *Shingles*.

In the Black Forest was inspired by a trip to Berlin.

Such a Long Life is a line from one of Gilbert's unpublished poems.

My Grandmother's Waltz was inspired by Ida Regenstrife, who emigrated from Poland to Winnipeg in the 1920's.

High Strung is dedicated to Lisa Tuininga, who paraglided from Tiger Mountain in the summer of 2011.

Acknowledgements

Grateful thanks to the publishers of these books:

The White Cypress, Cervéna Barva Press, 2011; *The Never,* Dream Horse Press, 2010; *Prisoner of the Swifts*, Ahadada Books, 2009, (Finalist for Washington State Book Award 2010); *Anne-Marie Derèse & The Green Parrot*, Ahadada Books, 2008; *Coppelia, Certain Digressions*, David Robert Books, 2007.

Thanks to the following journals, where these poems first appeared, some in different versions:

"Tribal Moon Cycle," *The Midwest Quarterly*
"Closed Head Injury," "Shingles," *Journal of the American Medical Association (JAMA)*
"The Phoenix," *J Journal*
"Anger," *Word Riot*
"My Father Returns as the Jack in the Box in a Dream," "Aegis," *The Stickman Review*
"Jacob's Ladder" *Women in Judaism, A Multidisciplinary Journal*
"Thirteen," "Montreal, 1946," "Cloisonné," *The American Literary Review*
"Cause and Effect," *The Mom Egg*
"Such a Long Life," *The Comstock Review*
"The Sifting," *Conversations Across Borders (CAB)*
"Wind," *Barnwood*
"Wolf Spider," *Bolts of Silk*
"House of Burnt Cherry," *The Pedestal Magazine*
"My Grandmother's Waltz, *The Chiron Review*
 "Notes for the Defense," *Willows Wept Review*
"Naugahyde," *Hamilton Stone Review*
"High Strung," *The Literary Review*
"The Skull" was published in *Many Trails to the Summit*, an anthology by Rose Alley Press.

My gratitude to The Centrum Foundation for two residencies at Fort Worden, where some of these poems were written.

To my fellow poets and artists Christianne Balk, Irene Bloom, Erika Carter, Eileen Duncan, Pamela Gross, Pat Hurshell, Susan Sigrun Lane, Anne Pitkin, Joan Stuart Ross, Joannie Stangeland, and Lillo Way, my deepest gratitude.

About the Author

Judith Skillman was born in Syracuse, New York, of Canadian parents, and holds dual citizenship. She is an amateur violinist, the mother of three grown children, and the "Grammy" of twin girls. She holds a Masters in English Literature from the University of Maryland, and has taught at University of Phoenix, Richard Hugo House, City University, and Yellow Wood Academy.

The recipient of an award from the Academy of American Poets for her book Storm (Blue Begonia Press), Skillman's also been awarded a King County Arts Commission (KCAC) Publication Prize, Public Arts Grant, and Washington State Arts Commission Writer's Fellowship. Two of her books were finalists for the Washington State Book Award (Red Town and Prisoner of the Swifts). Skillman's poems have appeared in *Poetry, FIELD, The Southern Review, The Iowa Review, The Midwest Quarterly, Prairie Schooner, Seneca Review*, and many other journals and anthologies.

Ms. Skillman has been a Writer in Residence at the Centrum Foundation in Port Townsend, Washington, and The Hedgebrook Foundation. At the Center for French Translation in Seneffe, Belgium, she translated French-Belgian poet Anne-Marie Derèse. A Jack Straw Writer in 2008 and 2013, Skillman's work has been nominated for Pushcart Prizes, the UK Kit Award, Best of the Web, and is included in *Best Indie Verse of New England*. For more information, visit www.judithskillman.com

www.ingramcontent.com/pod-product-compliance
Lightning Source LLC
Chambersburg PA
CBHW022009080426

42733CB00007B/541